WAYS OF
BEING

ISBN-13: 978-1548463038
ISBN-10: 1548463035

1. Poetry
2. Poetry Collections
Printed in the USA

For little nails,

The Flow of Things

5

Say What You Mean, Mean What You Say............107

7

<u>One Mic</u>

// One person speaks at a time \\

// Play an active role in listening \\

// Respect \\

Things He Never Told You
Bronx, New York

Behind the lights
the poetry
the degrees, fancy words and travel
photos

Buried deep between really cool socks
and things only tall people can do
are the things he never told you.

His grandmother called him boy boy,
in high school his nickname was
Rico Sauve, his favorite color is green,
but he hates to wear it
his life can be summed up by long days
and short years
and if chipotle was a person

I'm sure he'd have a new best friend.

He learned early the identity of himself
kindness dressed as, too many questions
with a side of, "don't worry I'll figure this
out"

He can tell when people make fun of his
walk
as if his swag was birthed by his
deformity,

He makes it work.
If split personalities had a face it would
be his
so a daily sacrifice of him-self in order
for the other to live is what he'll do

He's never been drunk,
never been high,
no tattoo or piercings.
so temple washings comes easy
when spray paint has lifted after tagging
on tombstones of ex-lovers.

He never quite got the hang of goodbye
I mean how could he
his heart
like hot potato
in hands marked for madness
until his hot potato, I mean "heart"
potato
heart potato
heart potato
heart potato, stops.

Never been
the Dumper always the dumpe,
so he finds it hard not to believe he is
trash. Taken out Tuesdays
wrapped in a black bag

A man of his word
And that word is sorry
or hi
or anything that would give him more
time with words.

He is a verbal guy so text messages are
more like fuzzy sticky notes on
answering machines
he talks to himself,
most times, in gibberish.

And he is the worse basketball player
ever, blind men make better shots than
him. tagged by Asthma, so yes
out of all the things he could suck at
he sucks at breathing.

He has trouble with moving too quickly
as if his thoughts play tag
play tag with his heart
play tag with his eyes
play tag with his feet
play tag with his hands
in a never ending game of hide and seek

He better watch it,
his pride has rips in it like fake business
man selling stocks.

so he's rippin himself on stage like a shot
from two glocks
and if he was a battle rapper he'd be like
big T rippin himself on stage with no fee.

Rippin it like a poet on stage wearing
dope socks
Rippin it like 4 stacks of paper in the
shredder box
Rippin it like Beyblades battles on a
school black top
Rippin it, like the Dead Sea as Moses
watched
Rippin it like overpriced milk at the
corner spot
Rippin it like the bboys in the 90s at the
train stop
Rippin it like cops writing speeding
tickets on the night watch
Rippin it like letters from your ex when
the lying stops
Rippin it like your pants to slim during
hop sock

He often feels like Adam,
A man made of dirt.
A Skipped childhood
face to face with his maker
and still puzzled by a tree,
A forbidden fruit called "himself"

So I'm super when im sayin it
pressed out kamemeha waves
as he stays
as he prays
as he lays
every ill gotten notion that he is less than
he always assumes the best even when
you hurt him.
and he never asked why
because he knew the how
so how could you...

As if blank notes speak in silent volumes
the echoes empty graduations
and high functioning depressing
and undiagnosed compassion
and no answers
and not holding back
and fear
and love
and waiting
and ambivalence
with weight loss
and weight gain
and closed doors
and open caskets

He can usually tell when people lie to
him
stories weaker than wet tissue paper
so holy the Catholic Church certified it

to perform exorcisms kind of lies

A backpacker,
an over packer
I mean how big does a suitcase need to
be in order to pack your pride?

He's learning what it means to be still
and how heartbreak
can polygon its way into Pokemon
shock like Pikachu, sleep like Snorlax,
with a fire-blast at every thought of the
past

He is often afraid of being wrong
but he's not afraid of correction
not afraid to check himself
wreck him-self
be put up on display
to say
these are the things
I never told you.

How God carried me through those
sleepless nights
how God taught me the meaning of
endurance, Proven character
and a hope that never fails
how God borrows my tongue to teach life
to a lost generation

How God doesn't care that I have bad
hand writing, or fast speech
how God sent his son to die for us
how God rose again to show us the way
how God is in this room calling your
name

How God is not in the habit of making
mistakes
how God mends the ties of broken hearts
and broken relationships
how Gods plan far outweighs my
imagination
how God defends me when my thoughts
wage war
so when the night screams pain there his
voice will Roar
so come death or shadows because

God

I know you'll meet there.

Bad Advice from Good friends
Queens, New York

It was a mistake to say you loved him
I don't think you fully understood what
you said.

And if you did, I know you tried to speak
it into existence but it just didn't work

Don't answer
Don't answer him at all.

He will move on, make new friends and
before you know it he will thank you.

Tell him one day he will thank you.

Any urge you have to connect is a lie
Don't believe the hype

The type
The type you be all around him
Turn the type off
Stop typing

You will defeat him
Forget he ever had life and spirit
You will step over it
Step over him

Act like it doesn't bother you,

16

Trust me it will work
Use simple language
To display simple cares

After all you're not suppose to feel
broken
It's wrong

And you've failed if you feel
So don't,

Breathe it all in
And pray it all out
Trust me
I know

Girl With The Name Tag
Queens, New York

Maybe she's just closed off
tell her how you feel
tell her what it means to have weight and
shine

Don't be afraid to count the memories
like numbers count everything

Move to the left,
or the right

Just keep moving.
don't point and stare
respond quickly
for your time is limited

And when she bypasses it
serves your portion like everyone else

You ask her

"Can I have just a little bit more chicken
in my burrito please"

Letter to Wally West
Paris, France

Time has not stopped
after all, the space between one place
and another is a matter of perspective.

Running only to be late
how fast is the speed of light
can I catch it
hold onto to the bright happiness.

I have been between rain
ran quick enough to not get caught but
slow enough to see the reflection of my
face in each drop

Do you know what it's like to stare at
tears in rain drops
like distant cousins meeting for the first
time over and over again.

I am no hero
not fast enough to keep them here
not fast enough to wipe my tears
not fast enough to touch those scars

I must admit
this is no gift
no amount of speed can outrun rejection
the color of sadness
the smell of forgotten memories

the taste of a blinded poem
the sound of a gentle hug before hitting
the stage

I am fast
but not fast enough to keep you here
instead I will jump worm holes to see the
end of May.

Preacher: audience of 1

Bronx, New York

Message i

Be an example of love

Message ii

I don't have to support your ideas to
support your wellbeing
we don't have to agree on the same
activity

Message iii

There is so much pain, so many setbacks
and discouragements, so many
controversies and pressures.

I do not know where I would turn if I did
not believe that almighty God is taking
every setback and every discouragement
and every controversy and every pressure
and every pain, and stripping it of its
destructive power, and making it work
for the enlargement of my joy in God.

Message iv

Exercise trust in Jesus's promises.
just do It
believe who he says he is.

Message v

Use the clarity that will surely fade before the next moment of temptation to build structures that will prevent this again.

Message vi

Hope is the confidence that the future promised to us by the word of the Spirit is going to really come true.

Therefore, the way to be filled with the Spirit is to be filled with his word.

The way to have the power of the Spirit is to believe the promises of his word.

Message vii

So

Me wanting to stay in contact comes from my fear that if too much time passes by where we don't talk, then I will loose her.

This just means I don't trust God enough to know that he will fix it how ever he wants to.

Me thinking I can do a better job than God is me reaching out.

Message viii

Be still.
Be silent
even though it hurts.

Stop digging deep into the past, it's just
me trying to convince myself that I can
fix it.
Be still

Stop trying to understand what
happened and just be ok that it
happened.

Message ix

I exist outside of me and her.
i am a loved member of Gods family
blessed be the name of the Lord.
find value in the Lord first.

Message x

How does this change how you interact
with God and people?

Message xi

Imagination is not better than Gods
sovereign plan for my life.

Message xii

Ask his will be done.
Ask him what does he want from me
Ask and you shall receive

Message xiii

Relationship may have failed but God didn't.

Message xix

And the faith-key that unlocks the peace that surpasses understanding is seeing him as the Faithful one and resting in his ability to do what he has promised. It is an easy yoke.

Message xx

Let us not forfeit this peace and bear needless pain.

Let us carry everything to God in prayer and trust him fully to provide everything we need

Believe that God rewards those who diligently seek Him.

Fully expect God to respond to your prayers.

Ask God to show you when you typically yield to selfish whims and desires during each day.

Learn how to be still and pay attention to Him speaking.

Message xxi

Pray that their faith would increase, that God would bring believing brothers or sisters around them, that He would heal and restore their heart, that He would make them more like Jesus.

Message xxii

I am beautifully and wonderfully made despite rejection.

Ode To Tall & Sexy

Bronx, New York

Night dreamer, a day light thief
running through text messages as I look
at my feet
unstoppable, feelings kept within me.

Couldn't see the light because I was too
tall and sexy
this side of me hindered all that I wanted
to show you
dance, poetry, film, soul, got locked away
in the back room with no air
tried to be the best of someone who was
too tall and sexy

Never could open the doors of my heart
so I settled for the window,
asked for your house as if that made
things right

By night I was away swept in the
madness of not loving myself.

How could I be so blind to the stye of my
naked eye in your heart? I was stupid.
took a chance and fell on my face, should
have stopped me before I set the pace.

Tall and sexy. Thats what I called it.
and i'm glad it has passed away.

No longer want to be tall because I could never see what was right in front of me. I was ugly

Because my soul treated love like love was no one. I was ancient.

Sexy was the pride of feeling ok on a day where ok meant tears. I was folly

But my deeds were done and I cast out the tall and sexy.

Back to the bridges I burnt, and heart I broke. With a note from God that says "Hope"

I'm confused.
unsettled in a settled down place

opened up that door and started the race out comes dance, poetry, film, soul. Old friends of a forgotten feeling I still want to share with you.

Big open spaces left in this heart of mine, waiting to be occupied, so I stand online.

Hopefully

Curled up with my words, they break me,
over and over again, He rebuilds me.

Molds me into the piece of art I ruined.
until i'm finished.

He auctions me off to the highest bidder
paying only in love. will you buy me?

Sitting on a steel platform with a gap
right before me. take the leap.

Flying over it is just the beginning, so
settle down because this picture is worth
a thousand smiles.

Crying Corner Of The 4 Train
Bronx, New York

Deep breath, just hold it until you get
home

Stand clear of the closing doors please
it's ok Mikey
it's ok,
it's ok Mikey

Maybe this is momentary
maybe she is feeling this too
maybe the numbness in her heart won't
have a clue

No, find a seat
a far seat
hold it until you get home.

Didn't see this coming
didn't prepare enough, pray enough
didn't know this would be tough

No, put your hoodie on, block your face
your eyes call the company of tears the
shape of brokenness.

That 1% Chance Of Hope
Vik, Iceland

She comes in the weirdest of times
makes peak-a-boo out of memories

Casts shadows on places you forgot were
there.

And you visit that old prayer
Crack open that old coffin where you left
her
buried her

You wonder if she feels the same way
If that 1% chance of hope will soon
multiply
give birth
resurrect dry bones

You pray
and pray
and pray
and pray
for that hope to live on

That she will feel like you feel and know
this bridge was never broken.

Perfect Attendance
Placencia, Belize

Always present

Here's a present

Gift wrap my gifts

Look sharp with

Make ribbon out of my life

But don't tie too tight

He is always present

He has perfect attendance

31

It Could Have Been Me

Bronx, New York

He kissed his mother that day
Funny
How good morning kisses quickly turn
Into goodbyes

His father worked the early shift
Gray jumpsuit of his own
Name tag and all
And yet still working the same streets
For 19 years

His father quit that year
Momma couldn't handle the pain so she
Needed poppa back home

His sister was never the same
Although she finished college
Changed her major from Biology
To sociology with a minor in African-
American studies
She fends for herself

He kissed his mother
goodbye that morning
I think he meant to stay
But officer mis-took him
For another Freddie Gray.

You Make Me Brave
Queens, New York

Brave enough to admit hurt
to embrace pain,
to love myself
to grow
to honor you

You make me so brave to climb
mountains and jump out of planes

You make me brave to call communion
with tears of joy and spell friendship with
prayers written on paper

God you make me brave to break out of
this habit of hating my writing style

Brave enough to muster up Spirit for one
final push

You make me so brave.
brave enough to admit

I lost myself,
Where I lost myself

Up The Barrel Of A Gun
Queens, New York

Flashing lights
see you running into the woods
backwards
in slow motion

And all I hear is anger
but my tears come first
How can I not be this black
this color to push back for badges

Can almost smell the gunpowder

Flashing lights
see you running into the woods
backwards
in slow motion

Click back
fade to black

Things I Say When
I Talk To Myself
Jerusalem, Israel

1. I am beautiful
2. I am beautiful even when I misspell
words

3. Sleeping is the enemy when I am late
for work

4. But Uber is my best friend

I like how pooling with people gives me
more moments to ride along in lives that
are not mine. Shows me life is nothing
more than an Uber pool with strangers
headed to destination pre-appointed but
I have no idea where everyone else ends
up.

5. I love myself, even when I hate myself
I love myself

Love how I think like
No one else thinks
How I am so happy with how I navigate
life although I am convinced life
navigates me

6. How the therapeutic process is meant for this body, meant for this skin, meant for this brown.

7. Praying to God like a long text conversation makes me feel more at home when I'm not home. How bible verse come naturally when I soak my mind in his word. His word, like brail to my heart.

8. My body isn't ugly, it just grows this way. Grow up my God says Grow up. And so this body did grow up and grow out

9. I'm allowed to love Jesus and fully be myself.

10. Talking to myself really doesn't mean I'm alone it means God is helping me to listen to voice when it cracks, when the pressure is on and I break. He turns up the volume to my soul so prayer walks feel more like skydiving from the moon to the projects.

Assume Good Intent

// It is not Personal \\

// Avoid Negative Assumptions \\

// Believe folks are trying their best \\

Dov
Nazareth, Isreal

His son would have been forty today
If he had not taken his life

Blessed to be a father of two
Grandfather of five

You never know the weight people carry
Your words cut deep

Add stones to my backpack
Keep adding stones

And when I reached the western wall
I will build the rest of the temple with
them, and with the stones left over

I will write your name in the courtyard
Spell it backward, and take you from past
to present

So you can see the stones you've laid.

High Functioning Depression
Toronto, Canada

How do you pull motivation out of its
hiding place?

Do you scratch the surface long enough
to see your name sketched in between
the scars

Maybe you have to wait,
wait it all out
wait for it to return in hopes it has not
forgotten your name

I make no promises

Only agreements,
written and signed by my soul

So by my soul,
soul bye my soul,
soul buy my soul

I Am Tree
Yonkers, New York

I kid you not,
I am just a tree

There's nothing special about me.
I don't produce apples or oranges

Roots aren't the deepest.
Not the tallest or the shortest

I am just a tree.

The first few days of my life I had
nothing but dirt on my face

Couldn't see nor hear anything
But oh the irony in Photosynthesis

funny

Waiting until the sun shines in order to
eat daily
Turns out
Growing and gazing upon the sun go
Hand and hand

Sprouting was easy
But water was uncommon

No friends to bring me buckets of water

The rain only held me for a day or two.

So I learned early to fend for myself
Selling body parts to birds

No one sat near me to read
Or played with my branches
No carved initials used to signify the love
of others

I am just a tree.

One who has matured enough to
understand my life has no value.

Screaming only begged the question
If a tree falls and no ones around to see,
does it even make a sound?

Sounds of a million ant march through
the veins of my iniquities. Building hunts
for houses the size of mansions on top of
skyscrapers.

Shedding the skin of my tears as I age
would only mean I'd have to clean up my
own leaves.

And what seemed like an act of God a
hatchet swung across my chest

It was the first time I couldn't feel my
roots, my gaze now only understood the
scuffs on this soldier's boots.

But 1 man is better than no man
Hacked into pieces
Bonded together as a symbol of
punishment for others.

I am just a tree

Bare
Broken
Bonded
Not me
But him

Tossed like a dirty towel before me
I think they called him liar
I think they called him devil
I think they called him blasphemer

He carried me, and although he carried
me I could still feel the weight of his love
baring down on my back.

Who was this man that I was planted for
him to carry me.

They say you can tell the age of a tree by
the circles inside so tell me

How many do you need to heed the
words of your maker?

Our fates crashed together in this
mayhem. I swear to you

I am just a tree.

I never felt the touch of blood before or
the sound of silence

Tell me

If an innocent man is crucified and
everyone is around to see

Does it even need a sound?

Crisis Theory 2012
Havana, Cuba

It was a long day from what I remember,
I took out my notebook and sat in the
back ready to copy down whatever the
professor would write on the board and
just before I could reach for my pen he
stated

*"todays topic, or other wise known as
heart break"*

I laughed because I felt as if I had been
studying this subject long enough to
have my PhD. With no student loans.

So as I zone the professor's voice out,
I pick up my pen, and write at the top of
the page *"Crisis Theory 2012"*.

First it was
Denial

that struck me like a silent virus mixing
my thoughts & emotions creating this
idea that things would all blow over
soon.

blind sided by my love for her.

Sat in the seat of my attachments.
Stopped at a red light.

but just because the car is on,
doesn't mean that its moving.

so of course every time I turned to
scripture it was somehow a confirmation
of us having to be together.
I thought that
if I read enough
and prayed enough
then God who is in control of everything
would fix this
would fix us
would fix me

Funny thing about denial
even though the word spells *won't*
we will still claim it says *will*.
It's not that we refuse to accept "wont",
but rather we can no longer identify with
its meaning and the reality of the pain it
bares.

Even my vision of your spiritual walk
became misleading.

Like

somehow you became perfect well
perfect for me. So when I was falling it
was ok, because I was falling for you.

I tried to logically break down why we
were meant to be as if it had anything to
do with logical.

with this
winters tale that would
spring shot us past
summer until we
fall, again.

Like a farmer miscounting his crops.
Because you reap what you sow which is
why you can count the number of seeds
in an orange but not the oranges within a
seed.

I would instill catchphrases within her
heart to remember me by like "If we
reach for the stars then we will land on
the moon" knowing that this could never
be because our universe of Love refused
to revolve around the *son.*

The Separation we faced had me stuck in
a mental prison, where my cell walls
were painted with every I love you. The
cushion of my bed made from every soft
moment we shared but not thick enough

to block out the metal springs of
disappointment that it rested on.

Because the hardest thing I ever had to
do was to convince myself

I'm not in Love with you.

If the beach was my life then I thought of
her as my sand, as much as I enjoyed
spending time with her I could never
truly hold her, because no matter how
hard you grip the sand

it still manages to fall between your
fingers.

It starts with the phrase *"We need to talk"*
which has the power to make you think
about every bad thing you've done in
your whole entire life.

I
just
wish

this pain would just go away

and somehow you'd stay
but as time passed on we didn't

And I grew angry,

I once heard where theres smoke there
fire

if thats true then I can't see anymore.
reality kicking in on this pain
I can't breathe anymore.

Because no amount of cast dice could

Clue me in this
Taboo of a board game, felt like
Battleship when we spoke, my
Cranium couldn't
Connect Four anything other than your
Chess like
Checkers, I would jump over anyone in
order to be kinged you were my

Uno that's the
Risk I took knowing it was
Trouble so
Guess who would be strong enough to
take this from me, he knew I would be

Sorry for all my misdeeds because I
finally understand this was not
Monopoly I was playing this was
Life and there's no second chance of a
Yahtzee like giving
Apples to Apples there would be no end
to this anger and resentment

we couldn't eat at the same table
I would see the cup as
half full
and you
half empty
but I wondered
If it was filled with poison and we both
drank it, would we end up in the same

place

So maybe I'd bargain with her in order to
regain control of myself, knowing all I
have left in my hands are

helplessness and vulnerability

Which is why I called her, every-night.
I lost track of the many nights where I
waited for her just to call.
Sad part is I didn't lose track,
I actually counted.
Counted every tear,
every late written text,
every pinky promise filled with anxiety,
every attempt at rebuilding,
every cry aloud in prayer with my
deepest pains being released with the
washing of his word.

God I tried to bear this burden of a
broken heart alone for far too long.

You God told me
Love Bears all things,
Believes all things,
Hope all things,
Endures all things.

All of which i've applied to my
relationship with her so tell me,
Is it me? Have we done so much that
things cannot be?

God I feel numb.

Like that day downtown when she told
me about the other guy.

Time stopped, yet somehow her lips kept
moving but it was as if my ears were out
of service. I could see the men by the exit
laughing at me as if somehow these tears
were unjustified.

I was low, so low I could look up and see
down right above me.

Back then I'd walk home in the rain to let
the drops cover my tears and i'd imagine
that God was crying along with me. It
was at those moment when I knew I
would have to accept it.

Accept our awkward friendship, that

"I use to date her but we're not together anymore" kind of friendship.

And now i'm sitting in class my notebook is filled with all sorts of madness so I have no choice but to turn the page.

And then it dawns on me Lord, The day they took you away. How Peter was so afraid of losing you he fought, with all his might swinging a sword defending you like a prized jewel. And that's not what you wanted of him.

God you saw your will for him and all of humanity as far more important than Peters emotional needs. Although you knew how much your disciples would be heart broken, what you had planned was far better.

So I a scared Peter have put down my sword.

God

every time you mentioned "us" I thought it was about me and her when really it was me and you all along God *us*.

Love bears all things; and you held me through it all,

Love Believes all things and I believe this
is for the best,

Love Hopes all things, and I know this
hope never fails,

Love endures all things and I have, but
endurance must do its full work so I may
lack nothing.

And just like Peter, I ran to the tomb of
my resurrected life to see

that He saved me
from having a
Crisis Theory
2013.

God Save The Queen
Paris, France

Ahh you!
a sociopathic javelin
aimed at anyone but you

A constant phase of me, myself, and I
tea party for one please
screams the queen
undoubtedly all her memories happily
obliged

Pour here. eat this, sit in your assigned
seat, sit up straight
sugar, spice, and everything nice
these were the ingredients to make the
perfect little girl

And it worked
perfectly prideful
young queen cuts off her own head
then argues with her body

she has finally met her match.

To Everyone Whose Ever Left Me
Bronx, New York

Thank You.

Battle Scars
Santiago, Cuba

I used and abused whenever I got the
chance to

trying to win a women's heart,
nah i'm not a romance dude

By 18 I thought I had it all figured out

I could just be in a bunch of

unofficial
official
relation-ships that sank to the bottom of
the ocean

swimming with no life-(guarding)
my heart
every time I spoke to someone because I
didn't want to leave time for real
(connections)
that were damaged because
I didn't have control of this drug (use)-
to be me but now
I'm better.

I was clean for about 2 years,
going through withdraw is so cold when
you have to deny the warmness of your
pride.

I understood my addiction well

Theres a shadow that lingered every time
I had to step away from them,
and even pushed away.

Can't seem to find the women of my
dreams so I break night thinking of the
ones I can't have.

Stuck on what if's and how come's.

Have you ever been in my shoes?
Shoes so wet from tears,
ripped from wars,
with no show laces because they stopped
fitting a long time ago.

I have,
used up every bit of emotion I have,
storing it away in the bank of a girls
heart, and as inflation rates rose I found I
had to pay more and more interest rates
until my debt was to big to handle and
had to file for bankruptcy of my Love for
them.

I was,
overly attached to the idea of a holy
marriage so every woman I met I

wondered if she was the 1 for me, while
trying 2 get around the interest in
someone else, got me feeling 3 times as
vulnerable, 4 these women that left me
with 5 broken hearts.

So I gave into the temptation,
started to use again

and let Satan hook me up on blind dates.

Where everyone's favorite color was
green

Telling jokes like
"why is 6 afraid of 7"

Distracted by facebook pictures and
status updates.

Sin had be buckled down like a broken
seatbelt, fornication hanging from my
neck like a chain that didn't belong to
me

I was wrong you see
to think that I had it all figured out

You see these battle scars

Cause by late night cuddle session where
my message was mixed, I needed my fix I
came back night after night.

Went on a shopping spree for my own
women, but you know the world and
Popeye's sell the same thing,
lots of Legs,
big Breasts,
fat thighs
but no ribs..

Everyday feeling like I was going to wake
up in hell

and the demon will tell me

*"Hello welcome to hell my name is tom, I
will be escorting you into the lake of fire,
please keep your hands and feet close
because you will get burned also be sure
not to scream so loud because its pretty
crowded in there"*

Hitting withdraw every morning when
my inbox was (empty)
is my mind when I get ahold of my drug

felt like Flying eagles but just small birds,
I was fooled.

To think that I made it.
When my eyes were just faded like a
burn out cigarette I was done.

My story was the same over and over
again

I was hooked
then clean
then hooked
then clean
then I was HOOKED

And when my half a relationships fell
through

because they always do you
were there for me Jesus with a giant sign
that said *hug me*,
and right below
I told you so.

Christ checked me into the rehab
kingdom where his blood was the
substitute to this addiction

but then
I met you on a Saturday,
you were the best dealer out there.

You wrapped my addiction in short
moments of
clarity
among calamity

Slinging rocks to the friends you've
made, I almost overdosed on you.

My addiction was just a gateway drug,
soon I had moved on to the big stuff

Adulterer

Things you cant find on your street
corner

fornication

relapse

Sin selling me different size cups

But God,
But God steps in and says don't eat here
anymore, for in my restaurant of love you
have free refills

Satan still telling me jokes
 like *"why is 6 afraid of 7?"*

Until I finally mustered up the courage to
answer

You see 6 was always afraid of 7

because 7 was perfect,
and created by 3

which is also 1 in the same being

he defeated 6 and his two brothers 6, 6

by gathering 12 just so this 1 could die for
infinite numbers of the world

Scars

Theres a reason why Jesus rose with his
scars,
wrote his majesty in the
stars,
my mind left on
mars,
and conviction got me up here spitting
these Christ centered bars.

So these scars of my drug habits are the
stories I will tell you,

in hopes that you tell me the ones from
your scars.

Conviction
Brookyln, New York

Seems like we've almost forgotten what
this word really means, or how it feels

its a life changing word for a sinner, but a
forgotten term by the saved.

You know

that overwhelming feeling of God spirit
slapping you upside your head

Or the sweet sounds of you crying at
night from your bed

                              Conviction.

like only opening your bible when your
pastor asks you to

sending that special girl a text and 20
minutes later expecting sex

Rationalizing your pre-thought out sin
and saying *God is loving He will forgive.*

                              Conviction.

Hiding your secular music in a separate
folder on your Iphone so, you, can scroll
to it in secretly

Or the pictures you've taken never be
distributed, only after you send them to
that special someone.

                         Conviction.

Deleting your Internet browser's history
so other can't see,
forgetting the mere fact that God has a
memory

                         Conviction.

Now if this word suddenly seems familiar
in your mind, just close your eyes and
you can almost smell the wine.

Of his blood

That was shed for us.
So he can provide that word that is o so
lacking in our lives

                         Conviction.

Like buying an engagement ring knowing
you're unequally yoked

This isn't Ihop there's no scrambling of
two different eggs,

because we are sunny side up before God
so if for a second you thought you was
well done He placed you into a separate
pan gave you a slice of his spiritual
cheese to made you his omelet.

You know its that too lazy to get out of
bed on Sunday morning conviction.

My bible is to big and my bag is too small
so that's why I don't carry it kind of

Conviction.

hiding your relationship status on
facebook so you can be both single and
in a relationship at the same exact time

Conviction.

its that I want to praise dance for God
but you have a twerking video on
youtube kind of conviction.

So what kind of life are you living,
because the one you've been called to is
greater

don't sit there and lie to yourself and say
the man on stage is just a hater.

You see, sin is a book bag and Christ took
it off us like the last day of school

We graduated together and received a
full scholarship to Heaven but you
declined
Because you rather work for a living, or
rather live for your works

So what kind of life are you living?

Because if you find yourself justifying
anything I've said then you've officially
remember the word you already read,

Conviction.

Like Shawn Hunter
Bronx, New York

You will never know how hard it is to be
disconnected from anything but can feel
everything.

I feel the pain to every cat scan,
see the lanes to every lap dance
that's why Ima Bane to every batman.

Ahhh you think darkness is your ally.

Cherry bomb Monday's blow up best
friends mailboxes.

Timeless turners become fathers.

And moms can disappear too.

No one left

So blockades can transcend seasons and
it will, as long as it doesn't scare me.

I always have dreams of the *Deathly
Hallows* stuck in his *Chamber of Secrets*
with no *Order of the Phoenix.*

Emotions escape like *Prisoners of
Azkaban* running loose on this Goblet of

Fire for a Half-Blood Prince of a brother
to steal the Sorcerers Stone of my father

Numbness for Novels
Queens, New York

Switch the characters
                    Deepen the plot

Even if you Mix and match the details

I can still hear the sounds of every page

Like I've read this story
Live I've lived your story

                                        Funny
How hearts can call plagiarism
On your played out story

Sprinkle just enough memories
                        To make
Me wonder if my thoughts would betray
me

Hide between the lines
        Smelt it from a mile away
                So, cast me a crusader
                    you were right

At least in some regard
As to why you would let me in
                            Well
    I guess I have numbness for novels

Don't Yuck
My Yum

// Agree to disagree \\

// What's good to me, is good to me \\

// Honor the effort \\

Morning Routine
Queens, New York

Wake up
Wake up
Wake up

                             Debate life
                             Debate life
                             Debate life

Late for work
Late for work
Late for work

                                   Uber
                                   Uber
                                   Uber

The Magic China-Town Bus
Philadelphia, Pennsylvania

Bus departure six o'clock
Bus arrival seven o'clock
Station smells of cold dragon breath
And spoiled floor wax

Driver   please   driver
Don't run us off the road
Don't take off before each person
Has sat within their row

O driver   please   driver
Help me know which stop is my stop
Which pop is a good pop
Bus hop the good hop

All worth the magic ride
Where there is a 40% chance you'll die
Contaminated bus air
All for a beautiful $1 fare

Sam Wise The Brave

Lake Ontario, Canada

I want to hear more about Sam
Frodo wouldn't have gone far without
Sam

Far as the eye can see with Sam
further than any man can ever be Sam
Where best friends teeter totter with
rings and armies

I can't carry it for you
but I can carry you

Meet me at the shire
Where the grass is green

And peace covers the lands like wool on
sheep

Meet me at the shire
a promise land for me and my kin
meet me at the promised land.

Hit With Chanclas
Bronx, New York

Mother, master of chanclentas
as if throwing foam feet protectors were
sport

She aims well
never missed the mark
they bend between doors
turn corners
they seem to always leave a sting

Mommy once through a chanclenta at
tomorrow and hit it.

Latina superpower
better than batman
stronger than superman
greater than green lantern
faster than flash

She is armed and ready for war.

My Fake Wife
Bronx, New York

Sends me fake texts that make days
worthwhile

Appointments for fake dates to build the
marriage

With fake hugs and kisses, we make it
through.

Remember the fake weddings
fake flower girl swings hand full of fake
flowers and fake tears down long face

Fake stories about first dates
fake proposals and fake approval
early morning breakfast in bed for my
fake wife

Who dresses the fake kids before they
are late for fake school
fake dreams of her at fake work.

                        For my fake
            wife.

A Sense Of Cycles
Paris, France

It was a cold winter night by the water

The sound of flashing lights

The gaze of left hand frostbite

The aroma of courtship

The weight of love

The taste of future blessings

The sound of three-letter words

The size of nearness

The tremble of eyes producing its own liquid

The sound of new genesis

The warmth of a personal letter

The echo's of winter chills

The sweat of fear

The memory of a forgotten tale too tall to set sail.

As Phases Pass Me By

Bronx, New York

I never went away for college.
the idea of dorm rooms and open space
always lingered in my heart.

Visiting campuses became reminders of
phases that have passed me by

I see rings on fingers that were once
naked.
like loved ones have moved on without
me

Reminders of fixed schedules and open
dialogues wasted.

As phases pass me by

Edited by Samantha White I

Queens, New York

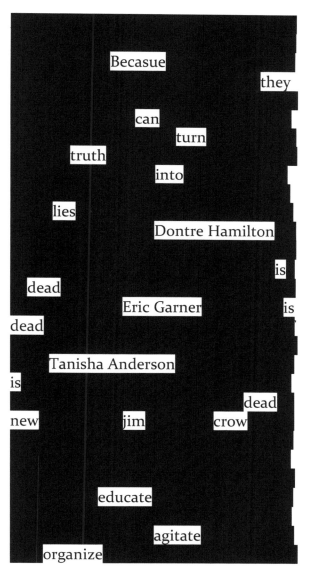

Becasue

they

can

turn

truth

into

lies

Dontre Hamilton

is

dead

Eric Garner

is

dead

Tanisha Anderson

is

new

jim

crow

dead

educate

agitate

organize

79

Out Of Place

Bronx, New York

Ever feel lost in a familiar place
step child of step child

Spongebob underwater fire
kinda out of place

Well I do
and have

Like costar outshined
like a packed closet of emptiness
truth is
I cant describe it

To be filled and empty
To be the center of forgotteness
I never quite feel in place

Birthdays are always tough.

102791
Bronx, New York

The awkward wait

As if feeling displacement only occurs
today

Midnight ballads of "happy birthday"

Today is always weird

The only wishes that count are the ones
you never get

As if today was made for you to feel
forgotten

Truth is I just want one person to say it

And I will wait in this prison
Orange jumpsuit and all

"Will prisoner 102791 step forward"

Yours Is
Paris, France

Yours is the glory
the pain turned upside down
where every knee is kissing the floor

Yours is the name called on and on
when rain has showered us with hope
a home too big for letters
too big for books

Yours is the way
the path that leads to life

Yours is the song that is written on my
heart
echoed on my tongue.
copied by my mind
and put on repeat by my tears

Yours is the change
the change that never changes
the flip flop of life
the other side of the coin

Yours is a Love
A Love
A Love
A Love

Slow Start
Paris, France

Find the key first
It's shiny red color should be easy to spot
It's not

The car has not started for two days now
so walking seems like the best option.

This model has run its race
the ink runs ready for re-entry.

No glitter in the blood can help
breaks of faceless facetimes.

I found the key
the car sounds weirdly amazing
like it was supposed to start just now.

For this moment here.

Move Up,
Move Back

// Practice Silence \\

// Provide Space For Others \\

// Speak \\

Tell Em'
Belize City, Belize

Tell em'
the mail never comes on time

Tell em'
Lord of the rings is the best trilogy ever
made

Tell em'
the third time is the charm
and the forth is a curse

Tell em'
tweet
hashtag
and facetime

Tell em'
folks don't care what you know
until they know that you care

Tell em'
seek first to understand
then seek to be understood

Tell em'
seek the kingdom of heaven

Tell em'
you care

you love
you can
you be
you be everything I need

Just
Tell em'

If I Could Time Travel
Paris, France

If I could time travel

I'd spend a day before the first day
would walk though the garden of Eden
looking to step on snakes

I would travel to try the first chocolate
shake

If I could time travel I would watch my
own wedding to remind myself I do
move on

I would stop 9/11, drop Hitler in a second,
invest in Myspace and Apple before it
was a thing.

I would travel just to provide therapy to
my family
give life advice to mom
hug my dad a little more

I wouldn't stop the bad moments
only trade places with myself so I could
truly save myself

I would travel back to walk with Moses

watch the devil get kicked out of heaven
and scream "bye Felicia"

If I could time travel I'd watch Tupac live
and leave myself love notes in the 90's
make friends in every generation
lead slave rebellions
and still make it home in time to watch
the Flash

Because that's what time travelers do.

Your Name Was Not John
Belize city, Belize

Your name was not John
not default
not hard to understand

You were grandfather
maker of boats
and journeys to flea market

You were chief and cook
were fun after bedtime
were mong beans and living crabs

I wonder why they chose John
was your face too hard comprehend?
your slum too low for public demand

Your name was not John
not blank
not commonalities and assimilation

You were craftsmen
Pick ups and drop offs

Your name was not John
Your name was not John
Your name, was not, John

The Things That Happened
Paris, France

The subway map.
The train.
The map.
The Selfie.
The false arrival.
The stranger.
The ask.
The borrow.
The phone call.
The French voicemail.
The following.
The journey.
The tea shop.
The smile.
The cozy seat.
The timer.
The hot pot.
The burned lip.
The tea cup.
The refill.
The tea cup.
The refill.
The tea cup.
The second smile.
The key.
The napkin map.
The Uber.
The poem.
The end.

Quarter Life Crisis
Queens, New York

Just me

Me and my quarter life crisis
stuck between full house
and boy meets world

And underlining depression of time too
quick to count classes

In high school
still can't believe I have a masters degree
and yet never missed an episode of
power rangers

My mind wants the 90's back
truthfully
i know it was my 15 year old self that
made me

How times after 9/11 shaped me
the music, movies and flow

I miss the late nights
before the date nights
when I wasn't allowed out
when nighttime noises mattered when
you had to sneak your favorite cereal
while moms was sleep

Shhhh
pour the milk in your room so you wont
get caught
hide the bowl
wash the spoon

Sidekicks for sidekicks
aim away messages still flow my mind
MySpace profile music made the day

When did I grow up
turned hey kid to excuse me mr

I still like coloring books
but I have this overwhelming feeling to
color inside the lines now

I cant seem to control my sleeping
schedules because I'm afraid I'll wake up
50

Make this quarter into 50 cents

Twin size bed time stories
summer days avoiding summer school
i've only ever been in two serious
relationships both ending in heart break
three cats
and one God

And me

me and my quarter life crisis

10 dollar t-mobile refills cards
for my boost, to boost my self esteem

I only truly loved myself when I was 15
i had no idea playing pretend can get me
a high paying Job
i keep traveling because I'm actually
running away from the fact that I'm
growing up.

And I don't want to
don't want my moms to stop waking me
up for school
don't want the feeling of newness to
become old.
don't want the feeling of breaking night
to become breaking bad
with me

Me and my quarter life crisis

I don't know how to rid myself of this
longing
And yet I don't want it to leave
do you know what it feels like to never
have to ask permission to cross the street
or cook late at night

Bring back the days where I didn't have
the keys to my house and my day
depended on the things I need to do in
between mom coming home from work
and leaving to school

So I'm left with this truth, my truth

People are growing up
times are changing

I pray these changes happen slow enough
for me to see it all
but fast enough for me to leave it all

With just me

Me and my quarter life crisis.

To God
Bronx, New York

A beautiful escape
a thought to think and remember

God you see me part by part
you fit me into boxes and ship me to
yourself to make me anew

And I still wait

My ears found your hands
sound of soft shock waves
you hear me now
you entered my life and broke the
brokenness

Only you can break things into place
smash into perfection
rip into whole pieces

And still I wait Lord

To be with you
a vapor in this life
a heart you've won.

This Should Be Untitled
Paris, France

Does it matter if I wonder if you're still
alive

Does your heart still beat the same

When like buttons are held captive and
postings are scarces, do you still breathe?

Is your face still like sunflowers sun
kissed sunsets

Are you still there
or anywhere
speak more than a few words

Fellowship with me through your screen
make friends with status updates and
check-ins

Keep me out of the guess box and out my
imagination

Por-No
Brooklyn, New York

One day a brother came up to me
he asked.

*If you got arrested for being a Christian
would there be any evidence to prove it.*

Without any hesitation I thought of this

This is a touchy subject.
No really it's literally a touchy subject.

Thoughts spark around 9pm then it
slowly works it's way up to midnight.
And by 2am I'm deleting my Firefox
history closing out every hidden window
so just in case anyone used my computer
they wouldn't have a clue.

No trace
of this chain
both hands shackled where the light
don't shine.
Getting off,
as I,
get off
these sites night fights end with me
asking for forgiveness.

Passwords in place,
turned of my Mac book just in case,
yet flashbacks off me failing to run this
race

got me wondering if my strength went to
waste.

So let me put this on blast every-time I
seek physical pleasure on the internet it
reminds me of my past.

And what scares me the most are the
mornings when I look in the mirror and
my past and present look so similar that I
can no longer tell them apart.

So ima tell you like the G told me!
Run from lust especially when dealing
with pornography.

When excitement comes creeping back
like fun in the sun remember there
is no fun with out the Son.

Because when I spell Fun S.E.X He
checks that's why I call him my auto
correct.

He is Constantly rephrasing every
thought being typed by my flesh.

Told me to run like Joseph
but I stay like Judas
get slayed like Goliath
when I'm suppose to be David
and when I read the scriptures I see that
David struggled too.

For so long I've been out of touch with
myself because I touch myself too
ashamed to come to God because he
could see through the websites of my
lies.

Conviction coming like a pop-up
reminders of these firewalls I'm headed
towards if I don't break out of this.
Por-NO, God when I see it,
I see no
but I don't say no
I react slow so
after contemplating I say go.

Taking Gods word like a joke

Fun fact

trying to defeat this on your own will
only strengthen it's grip like a hungry
snake deceiving it's prey constricting
after every failed attempt.

God you told me that I'm enticed by my
flesh when I don't draw near to you

so please send me your webpage of
strength because I've hacked my mind so
many times changing my IP address from
your house to mine.

I'm so led astray
I'm one click away.
Control
Alt
Delete

                        God please hear me
          Pray.

Worse Than
Paris, France

A feeling so hurtful
pausing to figure out what is worse just
to bring peace

Worse than vomit flavored candy

Worse than deleted essays before due
date

Worse than burned yellow rice
Worse than cereal and no milk, peanut
butter and no jelly

Worse than Trump for president

Worse than blizzards in Alaska

Worse than wet sneakers on rainy days

Worse than feelings with no words,
people and no passion

Worse than melted chocolate bars in
pockets

Worse than no hit ups on a summer day

Worse than train rides in the wrong
direction

Worse than ipad and no wifi,
wifi and no password

Worse than orange juice after brushing
teeth

Worse than losing all your contacts

Worse than lies from loved ones

Worse than me and no you,
you and no me.

The Time Before You Spit
Queens, New York

It's a weird paradox
Relax or rehearse

Silent or converse
With this hand gesture and that prayer

How big is the stage
Am I right with God

Stage left or stage right
Man what did I write.

Say What You Mean
Mean What You Say

// Be clear on your purpose \\

// Consistency between thoughts and words\\

// Consistency between words and actions \\

Avoidant Behavior
Toronto, Canada

Maybe later
like the student who misbehaves because
he can't read

Just call out
Like the employee who can't seem to
finish paperwork on time

Come home late
Like the parent who doesn't want to hear
the drama at home

Text back late
Like the girl who's too afraid to love
again so she doesn't have time to
hangout

Poem I'm To Afraid Too Write
Houston, Texas

There's this poem I'm too afraid to write

And it reminds me of all the feelings I
tried so hard to bury

To make peace with

Bargained with my eyes so the tears
won't be granted passage to escape

On The Trump Train
Queens New York

Legit not phased one bit

Like my people haven't faced worse

Like racism is something new

Like these scars don't have stories

Like my Lord didn't put these things to death

Like the train fare won't go up, again

Like my chipotle still won't give me extra chicken

Like I won't stop being awesome

Like "showtime" on the subway isn't the best thing ever

Like candy canes are made of crack

Like Obama somehow vanishes

Like Michelle somehow vanishes

Like history somehow vanishes

Like I somehow vanish

Like I won't still breathe Post Trump

Bus Driver Blues

Queens, New York

Real quick for all my MTA bus drivers
out there

What joy do you get by not opening the
bus door to me right after you close it in
my face?

Is there some contest among y'all?
what's the prize?
is there a championship held every year?
are there divisions?

Middle weight?
heavy weight?
by pass all your stops weight?

What satisfaction do you get in denying
me entry even though you are still at the
stop, being held by a red light?

Do you get reward points?
can you cash those points in?

Vent over.

How Hurt People, Hurt People
Reykjavik, Iceland

Like a void that needs to be filled

Your unprepared heart called mine to
battle only to self-destruct and hurt both
of us

How hurt people, hurt people

Passing it around.
i bet you felt ready.

Felt like it was time for this phase.

Couldn't take the time to care for me
softy so you opted to push me out
harshly.

Go figure

You hurt my hemmingway,
edgar allened your poe.
called doctor on this Seuss

To teach me
How hurt people, hurt people

Heartbreak Be Like
Reykjavik, Iceland

Organs on fire for dinner
be like a pro record of 0 and 365 all
knockouts

Be like zoom zoom zoom make my heart
boom boom my super nova girl

Be like missing all of your connecting
flights because you just can't seem to
make connections

Be like erased etch-a-sketch drawing

Be like selling engagement rings

Be like YouTube videos buffering on
internet explorer

Be like running away from your problems
to your problems creating problems.

That's a problem inception.

Stalker
Paris, France

This
      word

Worse than any other
      word
the triggering affect can make anyone
hulk out

Go super sayain at the death of Krillin

Send chills down spine only for spine to
completely reject it and force its way
back up

I want to understand how you can wield
this sword and slaughter a man.

The Stardust Voyager
Toronto, Canada

To the stardust voyager
remember to eat well
to set up times and reminders to fill ones
belly

Remember to hug tight the pillows when
chest feels like burning buildings

Guard your spaceship well for the voyage
is far from home, far from anything
you've ever done

Far enough to make you wish you were
back home
remember to cry
and breathe
and hope,
and call home

Remember home.
before the stardust settles
before the moonlight shines.

Remember your spaceship isn't broken
you just refuse to call it quits
but your suit houses a mighty God
A Holy GPS

But don't be foolish

this voyages can kill you
can make you date death

Stare emptiness in the eyes in hopes that
you go blind

To the stardust voyager
end this voyage.
go home.

A hero is not crowned by the voyage but
by the struggle to get back in his ship
and fly home

far far away
fly home voyager
fly home

Because If you lose someone, but find
yourself.

Your voyage is complete.

Sounds Of A Summer,
Fordham Road
Bronx, New York

Aye yo mami is all that real

Coco-cherry-mango

Free phone

Get your free phone.

Yo you, yeah you, you got a man?

We can't be friends?

Mami can we have MacDonalds

*Does it look like I have McDonald
Money?*

Man if I was a little younger

Bad credit

No credit

Free phone

Excuse me ma can I talk to you real quick

118

For the wages of sin are death

Ladies and gentlemen this bus is late so I have to shutdown and head back to the depo

Sighs.

Dear Snoring Roommate
Saratoga Springs, New York

1. I hope your dream is wonderful

2. My mind has already remixed your snores into rap beats, I just may have a hit.

3. I will bother you about this all day tomorrow, all day

4. I pray my presentation does not suffer due to lack of sleep

5. My lack of sleep

6. Turning on the air conditioner just challenged your throat to a noise competition

7. The air conditioner didn't win

8. Nearly dying to the sounds of someone snoring in order to get my Masters degree sounds just about right

9. I hope you know that I love you, even though I am upset

10. I can see the sun rising, I just may wake you up

Just Another Facebook Post 1
Bronx, New York

I remember skipped
meal
wet towel
chest pound

Like the morning sun
it set

Like the morning sun it rises

To bring forth light.

Just Another Facebook Post 2
Reykjavik, Iceland

If you could just peek into my heart
It'd
look
like Pandora's box flipped upside down

Packed
Labeled

Shipped itself back home to be around
other boxes that remind itself of un-
taped edges and unwritten notes.

Edited by Samantha White II
Queens, New York

I passion
Please don't shut
me out
They call us savage.
Mark
my face with

blood
of

my

blood

Spit of my
spit
You make me look lost
You make me look lost

Gunned down
News flash
system is

not

broken
designed
this way

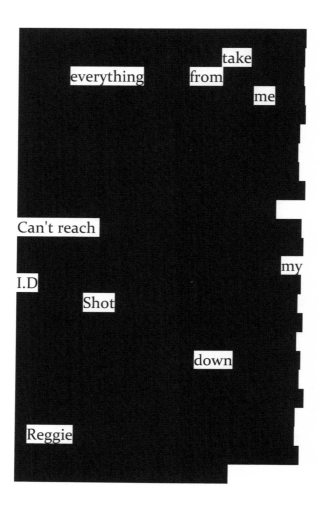

everything take from me

Can't reach

I.D my

Shot

down

Reggie

Fish Talk
Sea of Galilee, Israel

The fish must have said
Boyyy I didn't know humans could do that

I bet two fish got together
And made a bet

One said *I bet he drowns*
The other
I'm sure he will get pulled out

And they stared
Fish stop
Fish stare

To see a man step off his boat,
Walk on water and not swear

I bet them fish start to imagine walking
on land

Started to believe in evolution theories
Until they saw master
Master could walk on water too
In fact master made the water
And these fish

But still
I bet the fish made bets

Cast lots, measured the odds of making it
all the way

You know, maybe they held their breath
Started pitching campfires in their fish
towns to tell stores of humans walking
on water

I'm sure the fish must have said
Boyyy I wish I could swim on water
And another yell *boy! We swim in water*

But still
I bet fish made bets

They Make Her Weak
Queens, New York

They make her weak
Smell of this and
that

He made her strong
Pull up the pull ups

Only if buses didn't pass her by
Only if trains of men watch her
die
Only if planes can see her cry
Will she lie

And say

They made me weak
Smell of this and
that

They don't see
What I see
See
Black
See Meloene
See all the right things at the right
time
See water meeting body
See stars meeting moon

See future backslapping past to presently
wrap this present

                    They made
           her weak
                Smell of this
           and that

       This that too good to be true
           This that I knew what I
   knew
                This that you go boo
       boo

So I say

                    They made
           her weak
             And smell of this
         and that

Shoutouts

Thank you to my God, my rock and my foundation.

Shoutout to Kezia, your one random comment on a Facebook photo helped push me into making this book, and all of your answers help in such a big way.

Shoutout to Matt Strange and Robert Rosa for being brave enough to read my doodles on paper called poetry, love you brother.

Shoutout to the whole Truevoices Family past and present.

Special shoutout to Ramya Ramana, Chris Lilley, Canden Webb Cassandra Murray, & Leah James for inspiration. If I ever made a starting 5 y'all would be it for sure.

Shoutout to Jonathan for being more like a brother than a cousin.

Shoutout to J.L Escobar for the start and Delsy for the push. Shoutout to my best-friend Stephanie, you carried my burdens as if they were your own. I will never forget it.

Shoutout to Emmunal Nivar for keeping me composed when the pressure was on and the entire crew! #NivarEverafter

Shoutout to my sister Priscilla for being my tag team partner while growing up and also giving birth to the best little person in the world Ce'ani.

Shoutout to Josh aka Cut, you kept me on my toes, grounded, and reminded me that our ancestors have given enough.

Major shoutouts to Parker street church, Mami, Papi, Kevin Perry, Karness , Dr. Mazza, Dr. Monk, Dr. Mary Phillips, Amy Wagner, Maria Fernandez, Mustafa Sullivan

Shoutout Dr. Fabienne, the walks in the enchanted Forrest literally saved my life

Shoutout to everyone who prayed for me when times were tough, and I needed a way out. I know God heard them all.

You can support me by uploading your
thoughts of my book using

#WaysOfBeing

Thank You.

Made in the USA
Middletown, DE
07 June 2022